FIRST PEOPLES

HOPI

VALERIE BODDEN

CREATIVE EDUCATION ✦ CREATIVE PAPERBACKS

Published by Creative Education and Creative Paperbacks
P.O. Box 227, Mankato, Minnesota 56002
Creative Education and Creative Paperbacks are imprints of
The Creative Company
www.thecreativecompany.us

Design by Christine Vanderbeek
Production by Colin O'Dea
Art direction by Rita Marshall
Printed in the United States of America

Photographs by Alamy (Dusty Demerson, Pictures Now,
Chuck Place, Universal Images Group North America
LLC), Creative Commons Wikimedia (Detroit Publishing
Company Collection/Newberry Library/CARLI Digital
Collections; Pierce, C.C. [Charles C.], 1861–1946/USC
Digital Library; Pierce, C.C. [Charles C.], 1861–1946, James,
George Wharton/USC Digital Library; Tuxyso; U.S. National
Archives and Records Administration; Carl Werntz/
Library of Congress Prints and Photographs Division), Getty
Images (Scott Sinklier, ullstein bild Dtl., Marilyn Angel
Wynn), Shutterstock (Dimj, Everett Historical, Miloje, Emre
Tarimcioglu)

Library of Congress Cataloging-in-Publication Data
Names: Bodden, Valerie, author.
Title: Hopi / Valerie Bodden.
Series: First peoples.
Includes bibliographical references and index.
Summary: An introduction to the Hopi lifestyle and history,
including their forced relocation and how they keep tradi-
tions alive today. A Hopi story recounts how people came to
live in this world.
Identifiers:
ISBN 978-1-64026-225-6 (hardcover)
ISBN 978-1-62832-788-5 (pbk)
ISBN 978-1-64000-360-6 (eBook)
This title has been submitted for CIP processing under LCCN
2019938366.
CCSS: RI.1.1, 2, 3, 4, 5, 6, 7; RI.2.1, 2, 3, 4, 5, 6; RI.3.1, 2, 3, 5;
RF.1.1, 3, 4; RF.2.3, 4

First Edition HC 9 8 7 6 5 4 3 2 1
First Edition PBK 9 8 7 6 5 4 3 2 1

TABLE *of* CONTENTS

SOUTHWEST PEOPLE

The Hopi lived in the desert of the American Southwest. Their name meant "peaceful people." Other American Indians called them "the oldest of the people."

 The Hopi have lived at the edge of the Painted Desert for more than 1,000 years.

The Hopi lived on top of three MESAS. Several Hopi villages stood on each mesa. Each village had its own chief.

Within each village, people were divided into family groups called clans.

HOPI LIFE

The Hopi lived in homes called pueblos. A pueblo was made of stone and clay. The clay was called adobe. Most pueblos were one to three stories high.

Early pueblos had no doors or windows; they had just a hole in the roof.

The Hopi were farmers. Their fields were at the bottoms of the mesas. The Hopi grew 24 different kinds of corn. They also grew beans, squash, and cotton.

 Each clan in a village was given part of a field where they grew crops.

11

Hopi men did the farming. They also wove clothing and blankets. Some made bracelets of silver. Hopi women carried water from springs. They ground corn. Women built pueblos, too. They wove baskets and made clay pots.

 Hopi women wove images into their baskets and decorated their pottery.

HOPI CEREMONIES

The Hopi believed in many GODS. They held CEREMONIES for the gods. In some ceremonies, the men wore masks. In others, they danced with live snakes in their mouths.

 The Snake Dance was an unmasked ceremony that asked the gods for rain.

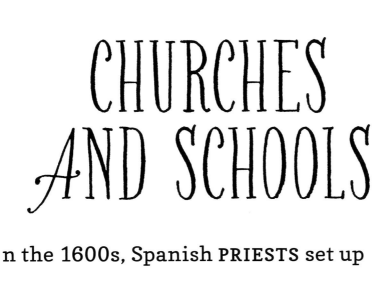

CHURCHES AND SCHOOLS

n the 1600s, Spanish PRIESTS set up churches in some Hopi villages. They made the Hopi help build the churches. Hopi who did not help were hurt or killed.

 The Hopi people were largely peaceful until outsiders began arriving.

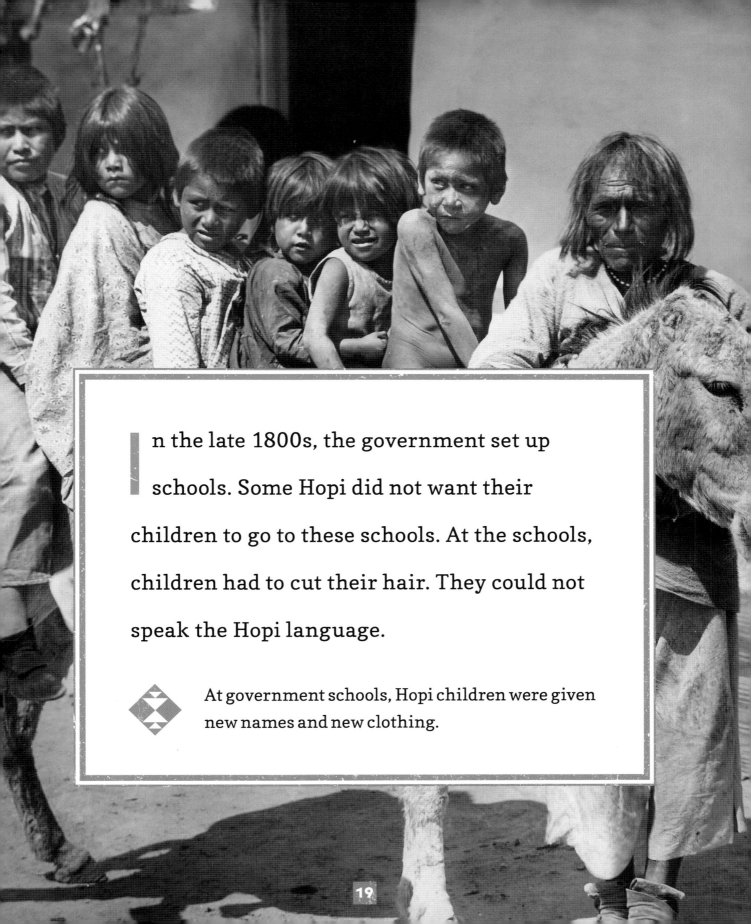

In the late 1800s, the government set up schools. Some Hopi did not want their children to go to these schools. At the schools, children had to cut their hair. They could not speak the Hopi language.

At government schools, Hopi children were given new names and new clothing.

BEING HOPI

Today, the Hopi still live on the mesas. Some still farm. Women still make baskets and pottery. Men still make silver items. They keep their TRADITIONS alive.

Many Hopi living in First, Second, and Third Mesas sell crafts to visitors.

A HOPI STORY

The Hopi told stories about the world. In one story, the world had become evil. The people needed to move to a new land. But the new land was high above them. So Chipmunk planted a hollow reed. It grew tall. Chipmunk chewed a hole in the reed. The people entered the reed and climbed up inside it. When they reached the top, they found a new world waiting for them.

GLOSSARY

CEREMONIES ✦ special acts carried out according to set rules

GODS ✦ beings that people believe have special powers and control the world

MESAS ✦ tall, flat areas of land with steep sides

PRIESTS ✦ people who lead some kinds of churches

TRADITIONS ✦ beliefs, stories, or ways of doing things that are passed down from parents to their children

READ MORE

Fullman, Joe. *Native North Americans: Dress, Eat, Write, and Play Just Like the Native Americans*. Mankato, Minn.: QEB, 2010.

Morris, Ting. *Arts and Crafts of the Native Americans*. North Mankato, Minn.: Smart Apple Media, 2007.

WEBSITES

Hopi Arts & Cultural Festival
http://hopiallnativefestival.com/gallery/
Learn how the Hopi continue to celebrate their traditions.

Hopi Cultural Center
http://www.hopiculturalcenter.com/
Read about the Hopi land and people.

Note: Every effort has been made to ensure that the websites listed above are suitable for children, that they have educational value, and that they contain no inappropriate material. However, because of the nature of the Internet, it is impossible to guarantee that these sites will remain active indefinitely or that their contents will not be altered.

INDEX